PIANO | VOCAL | GUITAR ▪ AUDIO

HAL•LEONARD
Piano Play-Along

AUDIO
ACCESS
INCLUDED

PLAYBACK+
Speed • Pitch • Balance • Loop

VAN MORRISON

T0087160

Cover photo: Photofest

To access audio, visit:
www.halleonard.com/mylibrary

5537-8672-5125-9584

ISBN 978-1-4768-1680-7

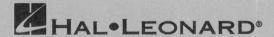
HAL•LEONARD®

Visit Hal Leonard Online at
www.halleonard.com

Contact us:
Hal Leonard
7777 West Bluemound Road
Milwaukee, WI 53213
Email: info@halleonard.com

In Europe, contact:
Hal Leonard Europe Limited
42 Wigmore Street
Marylebone, London, W1U 2RN
Email: info@halleonardeurope.com

In Australia, contact:
Hal Leonard Australia Pty. Ltd.
4 Lentara Court
Cheltenham, Victoria, 3192 Australia
Email: info@halleonard.com.au

BROWN EYED GIRL

Words and Music by
VAN MORRISON

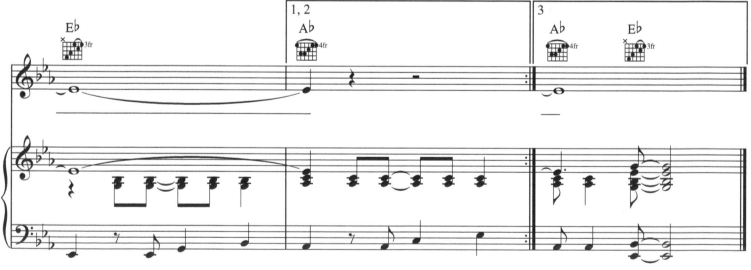

Additional Lyrics

2. Whatever happened to Tuesday and so slow
   Going down the old mine with a transistor radio
   Standing in the sunlight laughing
   Hiding behind a rainbow's wall
   Slipping and a-sliding
   All along the waterfall
   With you, my brown eyed girl
   You, my brown eyed girl.
   Do you remember when we used to sing:
   Chorus

3. So hard to find my way, now that I'm all on my own
   I saw you just the other day, my, how you have grown
   Cast my memory back there, Lord
   Sometime I'm overcome thinking 'bout
   Making love in the green grass
   Behind the stadium
   With you, my brown eyed girl
   With you, my brown eyed girl.
   Do you remember when we used to sing:
   Chorus

CRAZY LOVE

Words and Music by
VAN MORRISON

8

DOMINO

Words and Music by
VAN MORRISON

HAVE I TOLD YOU LATELY

Words and Music by
VAN MORRISON

Have I told ___ you late-ly that I love you? Have I

told you there's no one else ___ a-bove ___ you?

Fill my heart ___ with glad - ness, take a-way all ___ my sad - ness,

INTO THE MYSTIC

Words and Music by
VAN MORRISON

20

Too late to stop now. _____

SOMEONE LIKE YOU

Words and Music by
VAN MORRISON

Slow Gospel

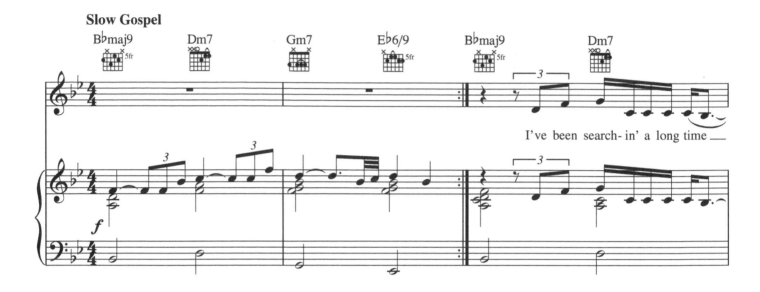

I've been search-in' a long time ___

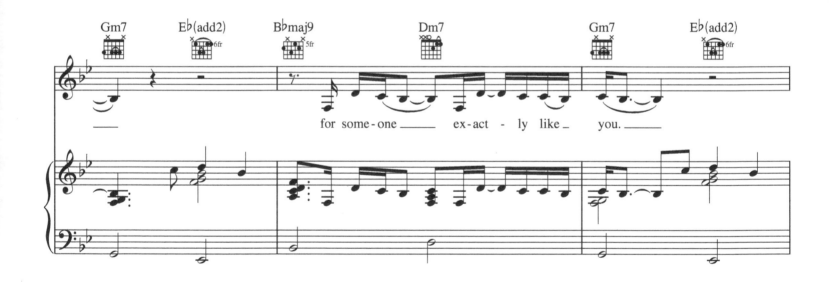

for some-one ___ ex-act-ly like ___ you. ___

I've been trav-'lin' all a-round ___ the world ___

TUPELO HONEY

Words and Music by
VAN MORRISON

MOONDANCE

Words and Music by
VAN MORRISON